PHILIP ROTH

IN MEMORY

Philip Roth

IN MEMORY

Remarks delivered at the
Philip Roth Memorial Service

September 25, 2018
Celeste Bartos Forum
New York Public Library
New York, NY

Library of America
New York • 2019

Volume compilation copyright © 2019 by
Literary Classics of the United States, Inc.
Contributor's remarks copyright © 2019 to the individual authors:
Joel Conarroe, Claudia Roth Pierpont, Norman Manea,
Bernard Avishai, Nicole Krauss, Janis Bellow, Judith Thurman,
Julia Golier, Edna O'Brien, Andrew Wylie, and Benjamin Taylor.

This paper exceeds the requirements of
ANSI/NISO Z39.48-1992 (Permanence of Paper).

ISBN 978-1-59853-660-7

First Printing

Printed in the United States of America

Philip Roth

IN MEMORY

Philip Roth: In Memory
is published with support from the
Crankstart Foundation

A Note from the Publisher

This volume has its origin in talks given at Philip Roth's memorial service. The sequence of the pieces reflects the program order of the live event, which took place on September 25, 2018, in the New York Public Library's Celeste Bartos Forum in New York City, except for the addition of remarks by Nicole Krauss, who was unable to attend. Some contributors have revised their remarks for this publication; others have chosen to publish their texts as delivered.

The proceeds from the sale of this book will be used to support the mission of Library of America, a nonprofit organization, publisher of America's best and most significant writing in authoritative new editions, including Philip Roth's collected works in ten volumes.

Joel Conarroe

Opening Remarks

GOOD EVENING and welcome, friends and admirers of an extraordinary man who was an extraordinary artist, and as his friend of more than fifty years I can tell you that his attention to detail was beyond extraordinary. As a result, I was not altogether surprised when some years ago—we were both relatively youthful—I got the first of seven letters, received over the years, in which he included instructions for his memorial service, listing speakers, the order of their presentation, and the music to be played. These go as far back as when both Saul Bellow and William Styron were included on the roster of speakers. The lists have changed slightly over the years with a couple of new friends added, one of whom, Nicole Krauss, regrets that a family matter keeps her from being with us—you can find her eloquent tribute in the May 24 *New Yorker*, which, I am told, can be read online, whatever that means. (I read "on page.") Philip loved music, and he could often be found in Carnegie Hall. I will return after we have heard from nine of his closest friends to introduce one of his favorite chamber pieces and then we will meet in a reception to talk and laugh and perhaps shed a tear or two about our brilliant, funny, courageous, irresistible friend.

I hope you will introduce yourselves during the reception, to my fellow presenters and to me, if we have not met. There are not many things during this season of our discontent quite so exhilarating, I would even say therapeutic, as talking about Philip and his books. Let me be specific: shortly before his eightieth birthday celebration in Newark I found, in a thrift shop, a Weequahic warm-up jacket. I wore it to the citywide party, much to the amusement of the new octogenarian—actually, I prefer the word *octogeranium*, my coinage. (There are a good many octogeraniums here today, and a few nonageraniums.) And now every time I wear the jacket, and I do mean every time, I hear "HEY, WEE-QUAHIC, What YEAR?" Followed by a lively conversation with, for example, Aaron: "I played center field—Philip will remember me, we lived right down the block." Or with Peggy: "My mother was his mother's best friend. I've read all of his books and especially love *Patrimony* because I knew Herman, his father. Tell him hello from Peggy and that I have eleven grandchildren." These and more, many more. I would then call Philip with news from the street, which always made him laugh, and if there was ever a more agreeable sound than our friend's unrestrained laughter, I don't know what it is. The warm-up jacket is indeed warm, and I look forward to bracing weather and more spontaneous conversations on the street about my favorite writer and dearest friend.

As official welcomer, I want to mention for the record a few of the many friends who meant so much to Philip. During summers I spent with him in Connecticut, I enjoyed getting to know his beloved Dr. Huvell, Arthur

Miller and Inge Morath, Bill and Rose Styron, Martha
Clarke and Philip Grausman, and others. And here in New
York I think of holiday dinners hosted by Paul LeClerc and
Judith Ginsberg for various orphans like Phil and me, the
delectable dinner prepared by Paul—Philip referred to our
host as Chef Goy R. Dee. It was there, on Christmas a few
years ago, that a great novelist got to know a great biographer, Robert Caro, and his wife, Ina, herself a fine writer.
And I think fondly of a reunion a couple of years ago with
Vartan Gregorian, former president of this library, who was
earlier at the University of Pennsylvania where Philip and I,
barely thirty, were in the English department, where he
introduced both his students and his faculty colleagues to
Milan Kundera and other Eastern Bloc novelists. The
Carnegie Foundation, where Vartan Gregorian is president,
made a generous gift to the Philip Roth Personal Library at
the Newark Public Library, which made Philip extraordi-
narily happy. The latest issue of *The Pennsylvania Gazette*,
Penn's alumni magazine, features an article by a former student of his, Jill Haber Palonne (students started lining up at
4:30 A.M. in hopes of getting into his class). After she gradu-
ated, Jill exchanged letters for forty years with Philip, who
offered support and encouragement as she went through
some personal crises: "His death hit me like a punch in the
face. I had assumed he was immortal. . . . It was only after
his death that I pulled out his letters and reread them,
reminding myself of how exceptional a friend he had been."
That describes the Philip we all admired—generosity of
spirit and a big heart. I suspect that his indefatigable biographer, Blake Bailey, the man he chose for the job, clearly not

an easy assignment, will see these letters if he has not already done so. Blake has spent time with my own hundred-plus trove of quotable letters. I will share a few brief passages when I return to the podium, letting Philip have the last word. Here is a preview: "I am making the commencement address at the Delancey Street School of Barbering in downtown Manhattan in mid-June. It will be on the subject of the page-boy haircut. I want to change its name to the page-person. But the powers-that-be down there are fighting me. I refuse to budge."

I want to acknowledge a few more of the many other friends who meant so much to Philip: hello to Richard Friedman, William Frosch, David Remnick, Don DeLillo, David Rieff, Robert Brustein, JoAnna Clark, Janet Malcolm, Mary Karr, and Leon Botstein, who gave us a fine lunch after the burial service at Bard College, where he is president, some weeks ago. I greet Susie Rogers, a wonderful writer who teaches at Bard; Mia Farrow, who could always make Philip laugh; Hermione Lee, here from Oxford, who has written brilliantly about our friend; Roslyn Schloss, the world's finest copyeditor, who made certain that his prose was impeccable; Nancy Crampton, who took such wonderful photos of Philip; Jack Miles, God's biographer; Barbara Sproul, who when they were together found the peaceful home in Connecticut where our friend spent so many happy years; Wendy Strothman, who as a publisher brought out *American Pastoral* and other memorable works; Chip McGrath, who wrote the eloquent obituary in *The Times*; Alison Lurie, whose marvelous fiction Philip admired, as do I; Susan Jacoby, who loved to talk with Philip about baseball; Linda Asher, his dear friend and widow of Aaron, his editor and special pal; Louise Erdrich; and Martin Garbus, who was in the army with Private Roth. I salute all of his editors and publishers and offer a shout-out to the team from Library of America, Cheryl Hurley, Max Rudin, and Geoffrey O'Brien, who made the inspired decision years ago to publish all of Philip's work while he was still alive, the third novelist so honored, following Saul Bellow and Eudora Welty. And who else had I meant to mention? Am I having octogeranium's senior moment? Oh yes, a president who reads books and who speaks English and not "Jerkish," as Philip opined about a man who will go unnamed. Along with another of my favorite writers, Joyce Carol Oates, Philip was honored at the White House, and during the afternoon before the ceremony Julia Golier and I were in a crowded room when the president came through the door and immediately exclaimed "Philip Roth!!!" To which our friend responded, "President Obama!!!" The rapport between these brilliant, deeply learned, personable individuals was palpable. I brought along photographs of President Obama putting a ribbon over Philip's head, of Philip and Joyce, of Philip with Vartan Gregorian, and of Philip and Paul LeClerc. I will happily share these with you during the reception. It was a glorious afternoon that Julia and I will never forget. Finally, one more name: a few years ago, I hosted a small dinner for Philip and invited my friend Warren Weschler, who had never met him, but who was, I knew, an ardent admirer. A couple of days later I ran into Warren, who shook my hand and said, "It was like meeting Babe Ruth!"

We will now hear from some of Babe Roth's nearest and dearest, to borrow Patty Volk's title. These friends will introduce themselves, but given Philip's love of baseball—we spent many a happy afternoon at Yankee Stadium—I can't resist describing Claudia Roth Pierpont as our leadoff batter. Claudia is the author of *Roth Unbound: A Writer and His Books*, a terrific work that he cherished. Claudia, the baseball bat, I mean the microphone, is yours.

And, fellow fans of Philip, I shall return.

Claudia Roth Pierpont

I'M HERE—as all of us who are speaking today are here—to talk about a great writer and a great friend. In many ways, these two beings were exactly the same man, and in some ways they were very different. Philip, the man, the friend, had the best qualities that those who admire his books would expect: a boundless energy and concentration; a fantastically antic sense of comedy and gift for mimicry; a quality of attention so intense, so penetrating, that no smidgen of pretense could escape it, or survive it. As a writer, he was a master, above all, of human voices. Readers of *The Ghost Writer* will remember the fictional master E. I. Lonoff telling twenty-three-year-old Nathan Zuckerman that what truly astounds about his writing is his voice—"I don't mean style," Lonoff says, "I mean voice"—and anyone who knew Philip realized at once that his perfect vocal pitch came from being a preternaturally attentive listener. Being listened to by Philip was an almost physical experience: the eyes boring into yours, the close questions, the unwavering interest that seemed to give whatever you were saying more importance than you'd thought it had yourself.

What was different about the man, as opposed to the writer—what makes it true that there were *two* Philip Roths, just as in *Operation Shylock*—is what he did with what you said. In the books, his purpose was to describe us as we are, not to take sides. People were always wanting to know which character speaks with the author's true voice, said what Roth really thought. But that wasn't how he worked. The job of literature, he always said, is to describe a problem, not to fix it. Real life, however, was different. If he cared about you, the caring was as intense as everything else. When I had eye surgery, Philip called more often than my mother. And he was intent on helping you fix anything you needed to be fixed; this was something he got from his father, as he well knew. With younger friends it might be sending them to school; with older friends, making sure medical bills were paid and life was as comfortable as possible. These weren't things he talked about. You found them out sideways, because he loathed even the possible tinge of sentimentality. And this, at least, was equally true of the writer and of the man.

Since we're here in this beautiful room, in this most meaningful building, which Philip himself chose for the occasion, I'd like to talk for a moment about Philip in New York City.

We all know how he loved and celebrated Newark, and his years of isolated work in his Connecticut studio are legendary. But in the years that I knew him, he was truly at home in New York, happily at home with the people here. He was—in his old friend Alfred Kazin's phrase—a walker in the city, for as long as his back allowed, and I was lucky enough to have done a lot of walking here with him. It was easy and natural to meet up for a walk, since we lived on the same block—which, of course, Philip called "writer's block."

We'd take a cab to Carnegie Hall, but we always got there early and walked around. Our best place to stop was the cigar store on Sixth Avenue, Davidoff Cigars, where the smells were so good and where he loved to interrogate the expert old guys who worked there on the decline of the Cuban cigar and the qualities of Nicaraguan tobacco and everything he could get out of them about their personal histories. And this wasn't for a book. He was just interested.

But my favorite experience of walking with Philip happened one summer day, a few years ago, on Broadway in the West 90s—Singer country—when he was stopped on a street corner by a middle-aged man, a fan, who soon veered off into his own story, as people, I have learned, tend to do. This man was a Korean War veteran, and the stories were many. At one point he interrupted himself, in an aside, to say, "I'm Jewish, by the way," and Philip nearly shouted, "I guessed!" While he was talking, a woman stopped just long enough to announce that Philip was her *husband's* favorite writer. The geography of Broadway in the 90s is important to this story, because I watched the woman go off down the hill toward West End Avenue while the Korean War guy was still talking, and then . . . I watched her coming back up the hill holding a cell phone in her outstretched hand. She had her husband on the line, and Philip took the call, and I swear I overheard the man say: "I'd come to join you but I'm stuck at work." We were on that corner for at least twenty minutes. Philip loved it. He loved *them*.

I'd also like to say something about what Eugenio Montale called "the second life of art": the words that come back to you on any given day, quite apart from the book they are in, as a natural and necessary part of your life. Philip loathed any whiff of pretention even more than he loathed sentimentality, and his language is so clear and deliberately unfancy that—unlike his characters, his stories, his inventiveness—it doesn't always get the notice it should.

But how often do I see someone young and think of him or her being "armed to the teeth with time."

How often, given the politics of our present day, I think back to *Exit Ghost* for reassurance, to recall how Nathan Zuckerman—who has lived through World War II, Vietnam, Watergate—reassures the young couple with whom he's been watching the election results of 2004, the second Bush victory: "It's a flexible instrument that we've inherited. It's amazing how much punishment we can take."

When I feel a sense of futility and loss, I think of the tiny, perfectly contained, almost Chinese-poem of a story of what Nathan sees, in *The Anatomy Lesson*, when, in the midst of a snowstorm, he comes to pick up the elderly widower he is going to take to visit his wife's grave: "On the front steps, in fur hat, storm coat, and buckled black galoshes, an old man was trying to sweep away the snow. It was falling heavily now, and as soon as he got to the bottom step, he had to start again at the top. There were four steps and the old man kept going up and down them with his broom."

In darkest times, in hospitals and cemeteries, I hear his words about his eighty-six-year-old dying father, in *Patrimony*, "utterly isolated within a body that had become a terrifying escape-proof enclosure, the holding-pen of a slaughterhouse." But I also think of his father sitting in the surgeon's office, fighting back the desire to demand not just a little more time but "another eighty-six years!"

I could go on and on. When I published a book about his work, I made sure that the quotations were in a type size different from my text, so that a reader could easily flip through the book and read a selection of Philip Roth's own words.

People always asked, during the last few years, if it could possibly be true that he wasn't going to write another book. But I knew how happy he was in his retirement, in his freedom—being "unchained" from his talent, as he says at one point about E. I. Lonoff.

In the hospital this last time, early on, before things got terrible, he surprised me by joking one afternoon, "You know, there's one good thing about this," indicating the room all around. Amazed, I asked "What?" And he said, "I don't have to write about it."

I'd like to end with two quotes from *Sabbath's Theater*, one about the beginning of life, one about the end.

> He was from the shore. There was sand and ocean, horizon and sky, daytime and nighttime—the light, the dark, the tide, the stars, the boats, the sun, the mists, the gulls. There were the jetties, the piers, the boardwalk, the booming, silent, limitless sea. Where he grew up they had the Atlantic. You could touch with your toes where America began. They lived in a stucco bungalow two short streets from the edge of America. The house. The porch. The screens. The icebox. The tub. The linoleum. The broom. The pantry. The ants. The sofa. The radio. The garage. The outside shower with the slatted wooden

floor Morty had built and the drain that always clogged. In summer, the salty sea breeze and the dazzling light; in September, the hurricanes; in January, the storms. They had January, February, March, April, May, June, July, August, September, October, November, December. And then January. And then again January, no end to the stockpile of Januaries, of Mays, of Marches, August, December, April—name a month, and they had it in spades. They'd had endlessness. He'd grown up on end-lessness and his mother—in the beginning they were the same thing.

And here is Mickey Sabbath's brilliant notion for fixing our biggest problem, the eternal problem that afflicts us so painfully here today:

Abolishing death—a thrilling thought, for all that he wasn't the first person, on or off a subway, to have it, have it desperately. . . . Turning life back like a clock in the fall. Just taking it down off the wall and winding it back and winding it back until your dead all appear like standard time.

Norman Manea

I F I WERE to choose among the many qualities and contradictions that set Philip apart from his contemporaries, I'd go for his obstinate rejection of banality, of the commonplace, of awareness dulled by the quotidian, where complacency, tribal loyalty, pious or prudent complicity, and collective blindness give birth to monsters. "*I had to squeeze the nice Jewish boy out of me drop by drop,*" he once wrote. Suspicious of parochial thinking or habits, Philip always "ran away" from any narrow, little routines, from bigotry, feuds, clichés, social hypocrisy.

Literature has other premises and potentialities as historiography or journalism, religious commandments or festive rhetoric. It looks at the human tragicomedy using introspection, phantasy, burlesque and ambiguity, and is anything but a vendor of cheap entertainment or scholarly escapism.

Nothing should impede the free exercise of the imagination, creative freedom, and the personal freedom that defies and overcomes the archenemies of original expression.

We should not forget that in the Sacred Book, biblical prophet-protagonists were so much a part of the tragic destiny of the Jews by virtue of their self-criticism and criticism of the sinful community. "*My mind is my church,*" Philip said. "*My laughs are the core of my faith.*"

We can, also for that reason, apply to the tireless and

increasing old-new anti-Semitism the words of a non-Jewish writer, Mark Twain, whom Roth admired: "*Jews are just merely human beings, and that's bad enough. Worst thing you can say about Jews is that they are members of the human race.*"

Though Roth enjoyed major international acknowledgment, he never won the Nobel Prize. Prizes are given by people and, like people, they are imperfect. Even were the Nobel to be awarded by computer, it would still be imperfect, as there can be no impersonal equation for such a fluid and vast and diverse spiritual territory. We can't even say it was not a bad thing not to win it! He thereby enters such select company with many other great neglected writers— Tolstoy, Proust, and Joyce; Kafka, Borges, and many others.

A thirty-year friendship between writers ("*a profession of vanity*," as Camus said) is not very common. But he took care of it even in the afterlife too, having written last year to Leon Botstein, the president of Bard College, asking to be allocated a grave at Bard, near to my own, so he wouldn't be bored, as he put it, in the endless "*beyond*." Now he awaits me there for our usual discussions about the autocratic new White House and the dangerous political meteorology around the world. Even about today's friendly and solemn gathering. The cemetery at Bard is nondenominational and even atheists are buried there. The funeral that took place on Monday, May 28, was nonreligious, in accordance with his instructions; those friends he had selected to speak were not to talk about him, but would each read fragments from his books.

When I reached Washington in the spring of 1988, after my escape from the nightmarish tyranny and misery of Romania and from my perpetual status as a suspect, and after my detour of two years in West Berlin, when we were in touch by mail, he invited me to New York, to Essex House, where he was living temporarily. I suggested we put it off for a while, because my English was too weak and confusing. "It doesn't matter, we've got hands, we've got eyes and we'll understand each other." He wanted me to bring him something translated into English of my work. I had only a too short story called "Proust's Tea," published in a London magazine. "Bring whatever you have." I crept into the big hotel, Cella accompanying me. Our host was sitting on the sofa, feet on the table, smiling encouragingly. I went forward up to him and handed him the few pages. Silence . . . "Proust? Proust, you say? I've tried to read this writer twenty times and I've never got past page twenty-five!" I froze. In Romania I had learned that if you didn't like Proust, you were outside literature. What was left to say to the great American? Nothing. I couldn't utter a word. Then another salvo: "Celine, not Proust! Celine is my Proust!" I knew Celine, he was an important writer and a well-known anti-Semite. I remained speechless, I smiled weakly and sat down on the sofa next to Cella, preparing myself for the next blow. But the conversation became more cordial, our Essex was soon out behind us. Outside, I murmured to Cella: "Finish! Never again!" The big surprise came when I returned to Washington: the American Maestro began to call me weekly, asking how I was doing, if my English was coming along, and gave me some names of American writers who spoke French to call them in his name.

My friendship with Philip deepened with time, each of us marked the life events of the other, and we always celebrated New Year's Eve together, in our home. Once he took me to Newark, where he was born, to see his childhood home and his old high school, the streets, the entire environment. He still felt close to the city. He had a deep relationship with the local library and a street was to be named in his honor. As well as attending each other's literary events, Philip and I visited each other in hospital from time to time, as we both got on in age. In more recent years we had had a grim competition for having the greater number of coronary stents: I was winning for a while, but Philip finally took the lead, with thirteen stents . . .

Our friendship endured, of course, all kinds of differences between us, perhaps well expressed at the start in the contrasting preference for Proust and Celine, but the connection was still strong, affectionate, and lasting.

Some years ago, in one of our usual weekly phone dialogues, I was thrilled by his good mood, his joy and optimism, so I asked about special news. "Yes, yes, I just brought home two irresistible kittens and I am watching all day long their never tiring game. I am really hypnotized." This reminded me of a summer sequence in his Connecticut swimming pool when he suddenly felt exalted. He was shouting: "Immortal! Norman, I am immortal, I'll live forever!" Two weeks after the kitten-show his mood changed. So I asked again about news. "I have to return my dear kittens to the store. I feel I've become dependent." Again, as in many other dilemmas, nothing should impede the exhausting and unavoidable task of writing.

Through Philip's fresh, funny, and ferocious scrutiny of intimacy and subjectivity, he offered us a revealing portrait of America over the last fifty years, its specificity and scandals and prejudices, its shallowness and energy, its candor, corruption, and cruelty. The painful solitude and dreams of the individual are always seen in his work in connection and confrontation with the taboos, treachery, and tragicomedy of conformity.

An acute observer of human existence, its cruel and burlesque conflicts and contradictions, has left us to face without him our explosive present and uncertain future. He will still be with us in libraries and schools and social gatherings, in the solitary silence of our reading rooms. If—of course—if our illiterate and narcissistic and lying president will not succeed in closing all libraries, newspapers, TV stations, and even change the too old Constitution.

Philip's forceful intelligence, his lucid and interrogative conscience, his unshaken devotion to the written page will still not be forgotten in our fight for truth and beauty, for ardor and authenticity. Literature, America, and the world lost one of the most brilliant great writers of modernity, an incomparable creative force. In the planetary political crisis of our time, overwhelmed by intense, speedy, and dark turbulence, we have to regain him on the printed page.

Bernard Avishai

"WHAT'S THE secret, Bernard? What's the secret!" So Philip would jump into many calls, in his most plaintive Willy Loman voice, our cheerful game, but not always, or entirely, cheerful, since "the secret" does, after all, elude us. Which is why he—or so the game presumed—was the roguish, striving, unsettled one, who wrote notorious, self-searching novels to prove it, while I played the square with solid responsibilities, married, faithful, *twice*, into the Zionist adventure, a political economist migrating to business to support my children.

"Willie," I'd answer, striking a tone of knowing concern, "tell me, why *didn't* Biff go to summer school?" "*Nobody dast blame this man!*" Philip would shout. And he'd laugh out loud, and I'd laugh out loud. He had played Biff in college and loved to mock what he called the play's "high sentimentality." *Dast. Feh!* Sentimentality was the plot against America.

Yet the first time we met, in 1974, it took him just a half hour, over eggs he himself scrambled, to induce the rawest of sentiments, which, I would later discover, he would never himself conceal. I was at his East Side flat because, *pisher* though I was, I had begun covering Israel from Jerusalem for *The New York Review*, and Philip was meeting me as a favor to Bob Silvers, the editor for whom one did favors. But Philip unexpectedly drew out that I was by then an orphan, that my late mother had been abandoned and unhinged, that I was in love with my baby son, a boy named for my own father, who three years before—life imitating art—*had* killed himself for the insurance money.

My wounds and obligations hardly made me wise—in fact, they made me scared—OK, repressed—a state of affairs Philip calmly determined to undo over the years. ("Bernie, are you in love with her?" "Well what are you going to do about it?") At this first meeting, though, my earlier life seemed interesting to him, which, for Philip, was the prerequisite for affection. Affection meant we might compare notes on "the secret." Do baseball uniforms arouse homoerotic feelings in *some* men or in *all* men? Can desire survive the joint payment of an electricity bill? You've read him, so you know that these were among the tamest of his notes.

You'd think that nothing would irritate Philip more than being reminded of the totemic Jewish men, an older generation, who condescended to his curiosity, men who denounced him, or, worse, winked at him, after *Portnoy's Complaint*—the Bernards, the Wapters, who purported to know what life's frictions entail, the keepers of a roster of do's and don'ts, a kind of secular American *Halacha*. Yet I can hardly think of a conversation over the next forty years in which he did not default, teasingly, to the voices of such men. They were our comfort food. "Not like that! You don't do it like that!" "Don't start-up, *whatdoyou* always start-up?" "Did you give it a courtesy flush?"

He adored these voices the way an antithesis loves a thesis. Voices that charmed customers, scorned bigots—

and beatniks—or sang "*Tzena Tzena*"—the song, Zuckerman's father proclaims, that was going to put Israel "on the
map." Philip's insurgency was molded by these voices. He
moved back from London for them. The idea that he could
thrive without them was, to use his favorite Yiddish word,
far-fetched.

Comfort was in conjuring the poise in these voices—
their appetites, obstinacy, routines. They didn't second-guess
themselves, unlike writers, who couldn't stop. He also
needed them for financial instruction, especially if they
couldn't "start-up": "I went to the cemetery to talk with my
father," he told me, probing to see if I'd agree with his father's
advice. "I sold the rights to *Patrimony* to a television net-
work for a small fortune. Now I'm thinking of pulling out of
the sale. They loved the book, they said. Only they insisted
on a few changes, which they figured would increase the
reach of the audience. First, they thought the father
shouldn't be a Jew from Newark but a gentile from Iowa.
Then, the son might be a daughter. More empathic. Then,
they said, instead of dying, the father would live." How small
a fortune, I asked? He told me. "So what did your father
say?" I asked. "*Take the money*; they'll probably ruin the
book anyway." Let's just say we both agreed with his father.

We visited Jerusalem together in the winter of 1988.
Intifada or not, he frolicked in bond-dinner romance.
"Look, Boinie, a Jewish sidewalk! Look, they throw rocks at
us just like Poland!"

It wasn't all hijinks. I took him to meet Ehud Olmert in
the Knesset cafeteria, the only Likud backbencher I had
liked and befriended. Philip asked him, without prompting,

just how the Likud government supposed it could maintain an indefinite occupation of several million Palestinians. Olmert answered that "if millions of American Jews, *good Jews like you*, came to settle the West Bank, then the land could become part of Israel." It was the only time I saw Philip lose his temper—actually raise his voice. "What makes you think we don't have lives of our own?" he asked Olmert. "You think we are nothing but candidates to be you?" The questions, Olmert later told me, stuck. Yet later that week, Philip and I sat in on the trial of Ivan Demjanuk, who had denied being the camp guard Ivan the Terrible. Philip scoffed: "When he was confronted, he called his accuser a liar. *A liar!* If you are innocent, you don't call the victim a liar." In Demjanuk's presence, Philip was, of all things, a good Jew.

Jewish voices, his first love, his practice swings. He'd move on to all kinds of complacent voices, from Republicans to French professors. *He'd* counter with self-conscious erudition, discriminating taste, scientific doubt, Eros, tolerance, sovereignty. The problem was, big-shot virtues prompted tragedies of a fancier kind: criticism turned to gossip, sex gone sour, private dispute become public, *savage*, creative fuel that blows up in your face—all unleashing (what he called in *The Human Stain*) the "persecuting spirit," including, crucially, self-persecution.

Which brings me to the darker side of his insurgency. Philip loved to quote Milosz: "When there is a writer in the family, the family is finished." But the unspoken corollary was "When the family is finished, the writer is bereft"—or as Zuckerman put it, "hated, reviled, and disowned."

The loss—all readers know—was primordial. The family home was, as Zuckerman said, "the best life had to offer." You were "protected, carefree, loved, obedient. Then came audacity, after audacity doubt, after doubt pain." Once, in a funk, he whispered a vision: "Bernie, you know that Sherwin Williams logo? I think the globe is dripping to the equator with pathos."

I'll leave it to the women in his life to explore, as Philip did relentlessly, what all of this meant to the women in his life. I will say that I once visited him in the hospital—let's say he was having heart trouble problems. At regular intervals, a nurse knocked on the door, "Mr. Roth, you OK?" His eyes lit up and an adorable smile broke out on his face. A woman's knock could seem metaphysical.

And if he had a lingering regret—hardly an unambivalent regret given the demands of his job—it was missing fatherhood. He famously could not manage even to care for kittens. But who can imagine putting up with the extraordinary demands of children until you have your own? Philip knew he had given up on something fascinating, absolute.

He once called: "Bernie, tell me exactly how you wake up a child in the morning. Tell me slowly, second by second." I later found the scene in *American Pastoral*, as lovingly rendered as the glove-making factory. Before his father died, he determined he had more money than he'd ever need, and so instructed his father to leave him out of his will. But then, when the will was actually read, and he was not designated an heir, he felt, so he told me, a stab of melancholy. He felt he had been hubristic, and in more ways than one. A Polish colleague, who had known Milosz, once told me, "Children get *beegger*, books get smaller." Philip loved that line.

His books, nevertheless, reported on a consciousness growing bigger, a life "vomiting art," as Zuckerman put it. For younger friends, he was our scout—bringing what was in the back of our minds to the tip of our tongues, revealing what was next. The manuscripts were always unexpected—puppets, boxing, Lindbergh, polio—but somehow not surprising. They pretty much seemed the by-product of our pilgrim's arguable progress. The one book that did surprise, which I could barely stand to read, was *Everyman*, his anticipation of his own oblivion. Now, alas, that book cannot surprise us either. Next is next. Life force, not a secret, was his genius. If Philip can die, then anybody can.

Nicole Krauss

I N THE fall of 2007, I sat down to try to write a letter to Philip, whom I'd never met. I'd started many letters to him in the past, only to put each aside, newly frustrated by my inability to write the letter I had in mind. But the more time that I let pass without writing to him, the more it bothered me that a certain long-standing gratitude and affection had gone unvoiced. So I explained to him that in his books I found a peculiar, sustaining solace. That, although there were other writers whose work I returned to often, no matter how much I loved them, they didn't provide me with the very particular thing that he did. What was it? This was the difficult bit to express. "I suppose it has something to do with a certain force of life that everything you write seems to throw off," I told him, "as well as the promise that such aliveness can exist in something that sits so aside and seemingly apart from life (or so it seems up in one's writing room); perhaps, even, has a better chance of existing there. Something to do with your lifelong examination of the writing mind, its needs and paradoxes, its incompatibility with so much else, and also its fierce pleasures. And it has everything to do with how, reasonably and unreasonably, I feel at home in your books."

I told him that I always found encouragement in his work when I most needed it. And what good company he had been to me for so much of my life. At the end of the letter, I told him that I had often been struck by a sharp loneliness whenever reminded of the fact that he wouldn't always be there, up in Connecticut, writing. "I felt it again," I told him, "when I read that you are now revisiting Conrad, Hemingway, and the others for the last time around. I suppose it isn't any longer just your words but their consolidated shape—the idea of you—which has brought me such comfort all these years, and I expect I won't know quite what to do without its reassurance."

A reply arrived in the mail, with a telephone number. I called. "So," he said, "are you at your desk right now?" "Yes," I said. "Writing?" "Finished for the day." "Good for you." "It had to come to an end at some point," I said. He paused. "No, it doesn't," he said, and that was the first time we laughed together. Plans were made to meet the following afternoon.

I arrived on the Upper West Side an hour early, wandered around, then sat on the floor in Barnes & Noble, rereading the beginning of *The Dying Animal*. Which only renewed, refreshed, and refined my fear of meeting the great writer, whom I'd been reading since I was twelve. As always when I'm nervous, my hands became cold. I rubbed them together so that I wouldn't shock him when it was time to shake hands.

And then there he was, already seated at a table in the back, and, after enduring his stare for a few moments, I was quickly put at ease. I asked if he had written that day. He hadn't; this was soon after he had finished *Indignation* and before he had started *The Humbling*, and he was still casting around for an idea. "It's terrible," he said. "I'm a complete amateur. I have no idea how to do it. How do you write? What is a story? 'Is this a story?' I ask myself. On the way here I found myself wondering, 'What is a novel?'" He had already written twenty-nine of them by then, but to him the process had not lost its mystery and could still evoke awe. I remember thinking then that *that* was the secret, *that* was how it was possible not just to keep at it for so long but to transform oneself again and again and endlessly reinvent one's art.

But it wasn't only Philip's humility that set me at ease. It was also his warm and ready laughter, his avidity for all subjects, his openness, and, perhaps most of all, the sincerity and absorption with which he listened. It won't come as a surprise to anyone that Philip Roth could really hold up his end of the conversation. But, between the stories and the reflections, the high jinks and the brilliant analysis, he was also the most generous audience one could hope to have. The joke he handed to Zuckerman—"Other people. Somebody should have told me about them long ago"—was never more ironic than when you were sitting opposite him, trying to answer questions about your experiences and impressions that no one else had thought to ask. This deep, attentive interest was fundamental to him, and was as pressing as ever, even after he no longer needed the material. Though, naturally, he still had a strong taste for it: "Have you used that? You should." Or, if the spontaneous good bit came from him: "Go on, take it. If you can pick it up and carry it out of the room, it's yours."

That first afternoon, we talked about our childhoods;

about the usefulness of invoking Benjamin Franklin when trying to sell life insurance; about Saul Bellow, Joseph Brodsky, and Sharpe James, the onetime mayor of Newark who was convicted of fraud; and about the regret, nearly universal among writers, of not having become a doctor instead. But, most of all, we talked about the intense, exhausting struggle that is writing. "I was hoping you would tell me that it might get better," I said. "Well," he said, "I'm here to tell you I don't think it's going to get better." "Thank you, Dr. Roth," I said. "That's right," he said, "your half hour is almost up, and that's your prognosis." That afternoon, I came away with a piece of paper on which he had written a short list of commandments to hang above my desk, the last of which read, "*It's not going to get better. Resign yourself to this.*"

I've been reading Philip for thirty years, and in that time his books have come to mean very many things to me. I may never have found myself in them, but I have always discovered myself there. What do I mean? Simply that, in his pages, I have not found a woman exactly like me, who thinks and acts and moves through the world as I do. But then I never went looking for my likeness there, just as I never hoped or expected to find myself in the work of Samuel Beckett, Thomas Bernhard, or Bruno Schulz, or, for that matter, Clarice Lispector or Alice Munro. What I look for in literature—insofar as I look for anything more than coming into a new or richer understanding—is the chance to be changed by what I read. Isn't that what we mean when we speak of being moved by art? The old position is disturbed; you leave in a different place than you were in before; in very few cases, you come away with the sense that you must change your life. I have experienced all those things when reading Philip. But my attachment to his work is born of something even deeper. When I say that I discovered myself in his books, what I mean is that, novel by novel, decade by decade, I came to know myself through them. When many of the struggles that his work so passionately grapples with came to be, as the years passed, my own struggles—the desire to seize one's freedom, to overthrow whichever limits and constraints, without abandoning that to which we owe loyalty and love (what strong, independent person wouldn't recognize herself in that conflict?)—I already knew, from him, a great deal about what it is to wrestle, and to persevere. Not how to solve the argument but how to keep it alive. Not just to withstand the discomfort and the tension of questioning but to make a life there.

And so, in the last years, it sometimes still came as a surprise to pass through the door of his apartment and find the man who took as an epigraph a line from Kierkegaard— "The whole content of my being shrieks in contradiction against itself"—sitting so peacefully in the late-afternoon sunlight. He would want you to listen to a piano piece by the composer Gabriel Fauré, which you'd do together, for fourteen minutes, each of you watching the changing sky through the enormous windows. He would be quick to joke, quick to recount, to explain, to investigate, to disagree, to hop up to get a book, a photograph, an old letter, to sketch a deft verbal portrait or do a dead-on impersonation, to press a bottle of his favorite grape juice on you, or a copy of a book titled *Galut* (which he wanted returned, by the way)—all with a sense of peace and fulfillment that would be remarkable in anyone but stretched the limits of credulity coming from the man considered the maestro of agitation. And yet should it, really? Wasn't it the nearly absurd but ultimately inevitable and deeply moving end that Philip Roth, and only Philip Roth, could have dreamed up? Wasn't it just like him, having wrestled for sixty years, having gone as far into wrestling as one can go, to apply himself, with all his intelligence, energy, and curiosity, to the other extreme? To peace?

On one of those peaceful days, four years ago, Philip rode the elevator down with me from his apartment, and as we descended the floors, preparing to say goodbye, he spoke to me about the shape of his days, and how he was sometimes suddenly struck by the awareness of being still present, still attentive, still alive. He said it so beautifully that when I got home I asked him if he could write down for me what he'd said, so that I wouldn't forget it. His reply came back quickly. I quote it here in its entirety:

> I think I said that I am struck by the fact that I'm still here. I become intensely aware of being aware of whatever I am reading, of whatever I am looking at, of whoever may be talking to me. It just seems to me extraordinary that I should still be alive doing these things that I have been doing from as far back as I can remember. I am still here, still doing. Sometimes, walking outside, I think that I have been walking under this same sky all my life. It's an odd and comforting feeling of posthumousness, that all this is coming after my life

but is still my life, a posthumousness achieved without dying. Maybe I'm saying that there is a renewed freshness enveloping me that is unaccountable, an emphaticness now lent to time-worn things, a constantly recurring newness just on the brink of its all disappearing. Maybe all I'm saying is that I know myself to be living at the edge of life, so that, as a consequence, something previously concealed. . . . No, this isn't it. Is it the fear filtering in as ecstasy? The thrill of still having what I am soon to lose? One is always intermittently stunned to be alive. Well, now it's not so intermittent. Years ago I stumbled on a phrase—I long ago forgot where—that captures, in its grandness and its vagueness, this situation in which I now find myself and for which I have had no preparation. "A full human being strong in the magic." I am speaking about a recurring sense of being strong in the magic at just the moment I am to be stripped to the bone (and far beyond the bone) of all the fullness I have ever had as a human being who lives in time. I am to cease being in time and of time, which is the ultimate magic. My last moments in time. Maybe that's the ecstasy now.

Janis Bellow

ONCE WE took a boat trip—Roth and Bellow wearing baseball caps, head to head, talking lazily as the boat drifted downriver from Brattleboro under a canopy of green. Not too many of these relaxed Monet moments in the high-voltage lives of two brilliant writers. But these weren't Frenchmen floating down the Seine: everything was quintessentially American—the two guys downing iced Pepsi, and laughing most loudly at their own lines. Ordinarily, they interacted like crossed electric wires: verbal fireworks in all directions. They had no history of easy drift.

Philip credited me with melting the iceberg massed between them after decades of jousting. From my point of view, I was the main beneficiary of the thaw. So much laughter—most memorable the occasion when Saul announced that I was pregnant, and Roth entertained the entire restaurant with an extended riff about how this kid would *never* make it to Harvard if I took so much as a sip of wine during the toast he stood to propose. Doubled over with laughter, none of us had managed a breath let alone a sip, but he was on a roll. (Try that again, and you can forget *trade* school!)

Saul was among the handful of readers who received advance manuscript pages from Philip, and he generously shared them with me. Soon I had reviewed a few Roth novels, and in 1995 we received a one-sentence letter: "Dear Saul and Janis: At last Bellow married a woman who understands me. Yours, Philip."

When Saul fell ill, he began to hand me the fat manuscript packages first: "You read this." I'd stay up all night, scribble on the envelopes, and quake when it came time to make the call. Philip took notes, he drew me out, at times he bristled, more often he was appreciative.

Philip deepened his connection as Saul's health deteriorated. No more improvisation or even conversation, but Philip could still make his friend laugh. Toward the end, Saul read only one novel, the one he called "The Book," and that book was *The Plot Against America*. Each day he would start again at the beginning.

There's a lot of kidding about Roth's attachment to his women friends, and the category to which each belongs. I number among the widows, a desirable enough group I suppose, since Philip proved unusually kind to the women his friends left behind. But Roth didn't keep company out of pity. He remembered Saul, "strong in the magic," and he never forgot me. When Saul was gone, Roth's manuscripts continued to arrive, with my name on the envelope. Philip became a dear friend, and a ferocious encourager. He'd wind up a conversation with a to-do list: 1) Read Beckett's *Betrayal*, and Nabokov's *Invitation to a Beheading*, 2) buy yourself a new coat, and then 3) a bolder imperative— WRITE! "in your voice as you are now." Responding to one of my reviews, he repeated the word "lovely" four times in a single letter and I knew it was "designedly dropped"—no chance of careless repetition from his pen. But he wanted me to move beyond reviewing, and urged me to jettison doubt: "You have to do it! Use your notes as a resource! Just tell what happened as the person you are now!"

For over twenty years I've taught a course on Philip Roth. It seemed he handed me a new novel every time I put together my syllabus. Tackling newly minted books made the students feel like audacious pioneers. We'd seek causes alongside the Swede, rummage through *King Lear* while studying *Sabbath's Theater*, and find ourselves the first class in history to see the characters from *The Ghost Writer* resurface in *Exit Ghost*. A startled student once asked me: "Did you do this on purpose?!" when he found himself reading *The Plot Against America* as our last presidential election unfolded. No—Roth did it! He wrote the book that made each class topical, electric. It pleased Philip to hear what the kids were thinking and saying, and I often called him after class to share the excitement. I'd be walking to the parking lot, and if he was chatty I'd take a detour through some falling leaves, and pause to write down what he'd said when I reached my car. I have dozens of these notes tucked inside the pages of *The Human Stain* and *Indignation* pressed alongside the maple leaves. When he felt high, he could share bits of a poem by Keats or slice the air with sharp remarks as effortlessly as Bucky hurling his javelin.

Student letters filled my in-box after Philip's death: "I feel I knew him." "He taught me how to think." "Reading his novels changed my life." I heard from kids whose faces I could no longer recall about the Roth papers they'd never discarded and the Roth novels they carted from city to city. Down the long years all that I had hoped to convey about what Roth wrought came back to me as gratitude.

In *Patrimony*, the story of his father's struggle, Roth memorably impresses upon us how hard it is to die. The story of his own life brings home a harsher truth: it's harder to write. Notice the portrait on the cover of Philip's last collection: six cavernous stripes between the impressive graying brows, the painful creased compression of the lips and a hooded right eye that glares out at you. . . . That's the man who transformed his life into a "slugfest" with words. We've read the warnings about the writing life: symptoms may include increased irritability, self-absorption, headache, heartache, blurred vision, heightened longing, and rare but extreme bursts of exaltation.

Roth described "the maxim that informed the writing of all . . . [his] books" in this way: "*all the assurances are provisional. . . .*" That "the relentless unforeseen"—without so much as a nod to order—carries off the people we love goes farthest toward undercutting any assurances. Here's Mickey Sabbath talking to his dead mother: "'Mother, leave me be. Shut up. You don't exist. There are no ghosts.' 'Wrong. [says the Mom] *There are only* ghosts.'" Your significant others—gone, disappeared, dead—become ghosts, but in Roth's universe characters continue conversations. As Mickey learns, we "imbue" ourselves with our dead, and they remain inside us, consoling, cajoling, blaming, cursing. They haunt us. Why? Because, says Mickey, "It's impossible that the dead should be dead."

Philip's characters never cease wrestling with their

dead—from *The Counterlife*: "I know now what a ghost is. It is the person you talk to. That's a ghost. Someone who's still so alive that you talk to them and never stop."

Now that Philip numbers among our dead, I don't imagine I'm the only one who talks to him. But who can replicate what he did when he buried his ear in the dirt to catch whispers, to eavesdrop on jazzy rhythms, malapropisms, and slang? He was playing seriously, and like Zuckerman, entering into "professional competition with death." It was a fight he relished. Fearless Philip carried each character up from Hades on his own aching back.

Aggressively irreverent, Roth gave us a lifetime of laughter from the trenches. Then, abruptly it ceased. In the spring of 2013, Philip told me, "I've recovered the life I had before I was embattled. The battles are over. I have come home. And I won."

And after the big fight? An interval before death—time spent on operating tables and in recovery rooms. But there was more. In a January 2018 interview, Roth gave an astonishing glimpse into the mind of the writer at rest. Take one look at Roth's reading list—his curious gallop, with detours abounding—through Coates and Cole, Greenblatt and Springsteen, Zipperstein and Akhmatova—and there's Roth devouring, at journey's end, more than most ingest in a lifetime.

Just weeks before he died, Philip entertained me, my daughter Rosie, and my recently widowed mother in his New York apartment. With a smile I choose the word "entertained," because I remember many a trek across the Park during wind and rain to stand before the doorman awaiting permission to enter the writer's lair. Philip, smiling at his door, backlit by all of Manhattan, in the long narrow passage hung with Philip Guston drawings, would offer a glass of water. He might be full of energetic questions and wicked gossip or he might be withdrawn. But nothing prepared me for the welcome of that final visit. Did he know it was a final visit? We sensed nothing amiss. He invited Rosie to play Bach on her viola, and immediately demanded more. She tossed off a composition of her own—he praised her profusely. He asked sensitive, sympathetic questions of my mom, speaking to her about grief and solitude. He laughed with us over a stupid piece in the paper—"You call this an art show?"—and snickering, read handfuls of foolish sentences aloud. He refilled our glasses with cool apple cider, and when it was long past time to go, delayed, and joking about the pleasures of having three women in his bedroom held up picture after picture of his family—the clan in black and white, his bright mother, he and Sandy in their cleaner than clean-cut boyhood. Back in the hallway, he lingered, describing the comedy of each cartoon for Rosie.

I play Philip's cell phone messages to hear his voice—at times weary, sometimes worried, often elated—but mostly because of the way they end—the music that signaled his goodbye.

I had called Philip to kibbitz about Bess in *The Plot Against America*. Like all of his mothers, she enjoys cleaning: working energetically while whistling like a bird. She inspired in me such a frenzy of scrubbing, I reported to Roth, that I hadn't prepared for class.

Philip's return message, his last to me, was "Stop cleaning! Those days are over."

And, of course, the coda: the long chuckling rumble of his laugh.

Judith Thurman

PHILIP AND I started talking about his death in 1983. It must have been early winter, because he was still forty-nine. We had met for the first time some months earlier, and we'd corresponded in the interim. But he waited for his next trip to New York to tell me some news in person: that his heart, as he put it, was almost "shot." He was still absorbing the implications, not only for his longevity, but for his freedoms and hungers—his life as a man. I was shocked by the change in his appearance. The radiant vigor he had projected, even bristled with, in the autumn, and his supreme playfulness—that gift for complicity which he tested you for at the outset of a friendship, then lavished upon you in its course—had been chastened by the only adversary that could humble him. Philip rebounded, of course, as he would from other illnesses and depressions—at times, it seemed, supernaturally, like those outsized rapscallions in the tales of Leskov.

Philip's vitality was so fierce that it was almost comedic, if you understand comedy as Leskov, Chekhov, Balzac, Kafka, Flaubert, and Roth himself did. The comedy of wrongness. The comedy of unhappiness. The comedy of angst. The comedies of lust, marriage, hypocrisy, ambition, piety, loneliness, betrayal, and deception. The comedy of tragedy, for that matter. "It's all error," Zuckerman concludes, at the end of *I Married a Communist*. "There's only error. *There's* the heart of the world." And then he goes out to stare up at the stars from his mountaintop, taking comfort in their impassivity.

If the specter of mortality haunts Philip's fiction, he could mock his own dread of it. He liked driving the back roads of Litchfield County, prospecting for a resting place the way other people spend a weekend shopping for country real estate. He joked about a "nice setback," "quiet neighbors," and a "tomb with a view." The majestic trees and worn headstones of the old graveyards we visited appealed to him, as his house in Warren did, I gathered: partly because it seemed so unlikely that he would end up there.

One measure of great writing, as you learn from reading Philip Roth, is its unpredictability. A banal sentence yields up its mystery without a struggle—you can anticipate the next word—whereas a magisterial sentence leads to a revelation. Sex, as Philip might have noted, is thrilling or not for the same reason. And, ultimately, he couldn't imagine spending eternity among taciturn Puritans. "I want to be with my own people," he told me on one of those drives. We had stopped the car to walk among the mossy plots where generations lay together, and he read their names out, as Sabbath would do much later. He was kicking a fallen crab apple toward an invisible net. "You mean 'your people' the Jews?" I asked. His eyes dilated with mock horror. "Not Jews," he said. "Writers."

There was a steeliness to Philip, a leanness of feeling. His affections weren't flabby. That sternness could be intimidating, though it was something you got used to, sometimes by standing up to it, which he appreciated. You see it in his portraits. What you don't see in them is his tenderness. It was Philip whom you turned to at your worst moments, and he came to your rescue. There were struggling young people whom he supported with wisdom and money, and some of them are here today. There were friends of his generation who might not have survived their bereavements without him. There were despairing lovers whom he talked down from their ledges—ledges he had stood upon. But I'll tell you a secret, a surprising one for such an adamantly childless man: Philip was a baby whisperer. I used to visit Julia's toddlers with him, and after twenty minutes of playing dodgeball in the dining room, I went home to write, but he stayed on, entranced. He once laid my wailing infant son on the rug in his darkened studio and, with a flashlight, turned the ceiling into a planetarium. Will was riveted, and Philip was riveted by Will.

I am sure Philip would have hated that digression into sentimental territory. I can see him rolling his eyes. He once described someone we knew as "braising in their own schmaltz." On life-and-death matters, Philip always hung tough, and expected you to reciprocate. In the hospital, towards the end, he woke up from a drugged sleep, uncertain of what was happening to him. "What do they call this?" he asked me. His gaze was like a searchlight. "They call it dying," I said. "Does everyone know about it?" He asked. "They do," I said. This seemed to satisfy him, because he nodded, then changed the subject. "We're expected at the Savoy," he said—that great London hotel he conjures in *The Counterlife*—"and we have to hurry, or we'll be late."

Philip's life force was never more imperative than at the moment he surrendered it. "I want to live," he said, on his deathbed. "But if I can't *live*—survive as myself—I'm ready to die, and you have to let me go. Even speed it up, can't you?" In that sovereign resolve, he was as lucid and as disciplined as he had been as a writer. When one of his doctors, an old friend, asked him what else he could do, Philip said, "Keep them away, now"—they meaning us, his close friends—"because I have my work to do," by which he meant the work of death.

It was Philip who first urged me to write about Colette, and when the biography was done, after eight years of toil, he surprised me with a gift: a manuscript page from one of her memoirs, written on her blue stationery in her voluptuous script. Almost all the text was crossed out by a latticework of fine pen strokes, like the wires in a pane of safety glass. The deletions, I inferred, were his message: "Kiddo, it will always be like this." The "this" was also neatly summed up in a line from one of Colette's letters that Philip printed on a Post-it and stuck, for a while, on his computer. "I'm hitching myself to the vomitous task," she had told a friend, her disgust as visceral as her will to persevere, on the day she started writing a new novel.

Philip, like Colette, persevered for six decades, book after book, their powers waxing as they aged. But neither practice nor renown made it easier. Philip, a connoisseur of surgeons, liked to imagine that, had he been one—a quintessential fantasy of writers—every operation would have consolidated his skill and his confidence. But, he lamented, "ours is the only profession in which it doesn't help to be an old hand." And nothing he accomplished in literature ever dissipated his sense of vertigo while struggling with a first draft, or his conviction that the vomitous task was impossible. My own sense of impossibility has always been nearly pathological, and Philip liked to tease me about it. "Poor you," he said, during one of our periodic discussions of his demise. "You'll have to write a eulogy for me, one day, and how you'll suffer! But it better be good."

These few pages are the only writing of mine, in nearly forty years, that Philip Roth didn't have a chance to read, to tear apart, and to improve. He would sometimes scrawl, "Good Girl!" in the margin. Or, "Now you're cookin.'" Or, "*All* of us come from somewhere else, so stop going on about fucking Queens." He expected you to be just as unsparing with him. He would give you the manuscript of a new book, then record your criticisms, so he could play them back. As you spoke, he took notes on a yellow pad. He might stop the tape to ask you to defend an opinion, but never to defend *himself*. And while Philip's talk—his inspired and sometimes wicked improv—could hold you spellbound, he listened like no one else. He listened with a primal urgency, the way you do in the wilderness, alert to danger, yet elated to feel your senses doing what they had evolved for. And he read just as he listened. And in his reading or his listening, you were heard.

The last time I spoke with Philip, before he shooed us away, I had just watched someone else die, a man with whom we both had a long history, and he wanted to hear about it.

The process, I told him, reminded me of a woman's labor, of childbirth in reverse. As I spun out the metaphor, I began to belabor it, and he frowned. His expression suggested that my loyalty, at that juncture, was misplaced: it was to love, not to the truth of a story. I was groping for an image to relieve his anguish, and I had meant well. But in the difference between "meaning" and "well-meaning" lies the genius of Philip Roth.

"That isn't so," Philip said simply. "At the end of a woman's labor, two people exist. When my labor is done here, there will be no one." But that isn't so, either, because he is still here with us tonight.

.

Julia Golier

"I DON'T LIKE to control things, I'm just thorough." That was Philip's response twenty years ago when to my surprise he informed me at dinner I was on the list of speakers for his memorial service. I was daunted by the thought of it and several dinners later asked if he might help me work on it. He didn't take me up on it, but every few years thereafter would send me an updated list of the memorial speakers and the precise order in which we were to speak, along with a copy of his health care proxy and living will.

I started seeing Philip in 1994. We ran into each other on Park Avenue one evening. I was walking home from work and he had just dropped off the manuscript of *Sabbath's Theater* with his agent, Andrew Wylie. Philip and I had met previously and another time he tracked me down at the VA hospital to get some information for a book he was writing. We were at very different stages of life; I was completing a psychiatry research fellowship and he was dealing with the dissolution of his second marriage. But somehow at dinner that night we found all the same things funny and there began a very playful relationship.

It would become a haven from other realities for both of us for the next few years, during which he did some of his most important work and I made some of my most important life decisions. We would remain a steadying influence on each other for over two decades. "Who would have thunk it?" Philip said.

He first invited me to spend a weekend at his Connecticut home in 1995. He had a plan that was well under way to build a new one-story house and sell his old farmhouse and the adjacent studio, to move forward in his life. He had planted a wall of pines to block the view of the old house from that of his new house. He had the architect's model of the new house; he loved opening and closing its little cardboard doors. The excavator was coming that Monday to cut a new road to the building site. But when I arrived, I was stunned. "You can't get rid of this beautiful house," I told him. "Hard as it is to believe, I have come to hate this house," he said. "And not *only* do I hate the house, I also hate the two-hundred-year-old maple and ash trees that shade it." I don't know where I got my resolve, I was still wondering what I was even doing at Philip Roth's country home, but I persisted all the same. I took him room by room to make him believe there were many good years ahead. By Sunday night he sullenly acquiesced, "Fine, I'll keep the house."

I spent as much time with him there as I could over the next few years. We had a very private life, which was serene and ordinary and full of simple routines, the details of which might bore you. His driver picked me up from the Wingdale train station every Friday night, and when I arrived, Philip always had dinner ready for me and on the table—usually fresh fish from the seafood truck in Kent, corn, and tomatoes. Next to my plate he placed newspaper clippings or interesting mail from the week. Philip loved everything about mail, mailing things, and the U.S. Postal Service.

Every single day, after breakfast and morning calisthenics, he went straight to the studio to write. There was no decision to be made about this; writing was his job and his boss was unreasonable. In the afternoons, we walked along the river—"There's no tonic like the Housatonic," he would say. At night we gazed at the stars over the plowed fields and played gin rummy at the kitchen table. He tracked his cards very closely but would try to fool you, saying "I've got a hand like a foot." And every Saturday night in the living room of the house he no longer hated we listened to Susan Kennedy of WMNR Fine Arts Radio play the great songs and sweet sounds of the Big Band Era. During this time, we rarely saw anyone or went anywhere. In me he had found someone for whom this didn't much matter. As Philip used to say, "Salman Rushdie leaves his house more than you do." But together we couldn't have been happier.

American Pastoral was written against this calm backdrop. So was *I Married a Communist*, but after a little bit of turbulence. One of those summers we became fascinated by wildflowers. We walked all over Litchfield County in high boots carrying *Peterson's Field Guide* so we could identify them by name. Chicory, pasture thistle, wild pinks, and joe-pye weed. These were the names of the flowers Merry Levov would learn about at her 4-H club in Old Rimrock, a small detail that the Swede would recall the day she reappeared to tell her grandfather that the death toll was four.

Regarding that masterpiece, I am embarrassed to admit that I tried to convince Philip to change its title. On a ride back to New York City he strenuously defended it to me: "I have earned the right to call it *American Pastoral*," he said. I didn't fully grasp what he meant then, but it is clear to me now. I should also tell you that it almost wasn't published. He called Andrew in London one night and told him to halt publication. He was done with writing; the deal was off. A series of dizzying and comical phone calls ensued— and saved that year's selection for the Pulitzer Prize.

I was fortunate to accompany him when he received that award, as well as when he was honored at the White House, twice, and at a wonderful literary festival, The Roth Explosion, in Aix-en-Provence, filled with master classes, panel discussions, music, and film. In Aix, bright red over-sized banners of his head were hung throughout the village. He told the audience, "Now I know what it is like to be Chairman Mao." When he walked through the village teenage girls came up to him screaming "Philip Roth, Philip Roth." But what delighted him more than being treated like a rock star was being in a place where ordinary citizens came out night after night to talk about literature.

Eventually it was time for me to move on to the life I had hoped for and was destined to lead. Philip encouraged and stood by me. Fortunately, I would meet my husband, Bill Bornmann, following another chance encounter, this time on East 91st. The Upper East Side has been good to me, but that is a story for another day.

Bill and I welcomed William and Amelia into our lives in 2003. I thought Philip might naturally distance himself from us then, that he would be bored by the babies and the chatter of new parents. But when he first visited the twins, he plainly fell in love. When they were babies, he and Judith Thurman would come visit them while we were at work. She would stay the normal amount of time that you visit someone else's cute kids, and he would stay on for hours. When they were older, they would enjoy Philip's magic—he would watch them from the side of his pool and cheer on their dives and pirouettes, introduce them to Fred and Ginger movies, and tell them his favorite joke about Hawaii. Depending on the season, he and William would cheer on the Yankees together or bet against each other on the Super Bowl.

Not long after Philip secretly retired, Amelia sent him a simple note: "I was thinking about books and I wonder if I could write a book with you." With that they began writing little stories in tandem, providing alternating lines by email, with him coaxing her along. They wrote about stars, and animals, and girls who dream big; they were like typical children's stories but sometimes veered off to some of Philip's favorite concerns. He defined a new malady, ISN, which stands for Inescapable Snail Narcissism, to describe what overcomes Oppy and Pessy when they get their outer shells buffed and shined at the snail salon. In the story about Benjamin and Bernice, two dogs who go to medical school, we get a critique of bark therapy after they inevitably meet Dr. Floyd. Philip described in another story how families of monkeys arrived by the truckload at the Bornmanns' house to live in their basement. With that, Amelia didn't skip a beat. She inserted Philip Roth into the story, as a character writing a book about monkeys, at which point I thought: My God, he has highjacked my daughter.

The twins brought him a lot of joy; I recently found he had saved all the cards they had made for him. Perhaps I shouldn't have been as surprised as I was that in the end this is the story of how the childless novelist became a grandfather. When Philip first came to Thanksgiving at my parents' house, many years earlier, he effortlessly honored my father's request to say grace before dinner. He began, as the Swede did, with, "I am not a religious man, but when I look around this table, I know that something is shining down on me." He meant it. A part of him had always longed for family life. He last visited with us on Easter, which he loved. He was delighted by the cousins and their baskets and bunnies. He hadn't looked better in years. When he blew out all the candles on the birthday cake we had for him, we mistook it as a sign of longevity.

Several weeks later he was in the CCU. I called my mother from his room when the outcome was becoming clearer; she gave me her loving advice: "You should baptize him," she said. "All you need is water and this way you will be sure he goes straight to Heaven." I ran it by him. He considered it, but declined. "I don't think all the really fun people will be in Heaven. And besides, I think the people in charge of these things will get me to where I need to go."

I don't know where he went, but I can tell you that wherever it is, he went there as a happy man, confident that he had lived the life he was meant to live.

.

Edna O'Brien

The Great Comic Literary Conquistador

I N HER poem, "One need not be a chamber to be haunted," Emily Dickinson wrote of the mind's many niches and the spectral encounters of night. I have been thinking of the forbidding rooms of Philip Roth, a man so studiously private in life, and as an author zanily, volubly confessional. He set forth his own manifesto in a few terse words: "Fiction is not a beauty contest and fiction is not autobiography." Were he to write an autobiography, he maintained, it would make Beckett's *The Unnamable* read like one of the rich narratives of Charles Dickens.

"I read fiction," he wrote, "to be free of my own suffo-catingly boring and narrow perspective on life, and to be lured into imaginative sympathy with a fully developed narrative and point of view. It is for the very same reason I write it." His inclination was towards the loopy, the carni-valesque, the aggressive, the clownlike, and filled with the titanic indiscretions that he so admired in Saul Bellow's *Henderson the Rain King*.

So, the Parental Room. A family of four: father, mother, and two sons, one the putative writer, both rebellious and bedeviled by long-standing loyalties. "A Jewish man," he would go on to say, "with his parents alive is half of the time a helpless infant. Listen. Come to my aid. Spring me from the role of the smothered son." The other half of him did spring to become the great comic literary conquistador.

He loved his parents, his father who was dogmatic, unswerving, but with limitless pride in his son. A father who showed great stoicism after a financial setback in his mid-forties, and to Philip seemed an amalgam of Captain Ahab and Willy Loman. He feared more than anything that he would disappoint both his parents, that he would in fact break their hearts.

His relationship with his mother is more intricate. She remained the secret siren, perpetually curled up inside him. She was self-effacing, yet had her own particular witchcraft, so that she could pass through windows or concoct stratagems from her apron pocket. Up to the age of five—before he went to school—they were alone, blissfully alone; he, the little kitchen jester, doing impersonations of Jack Benny and other popular television characters, and she, though in ripples of laughter, convinced that she had given birth to another Albert Einstein. So umbilical, abiding, and intermeshed was this relationship with mother, that when Philip had a coronary bypass in middle age, he invites us to witness his beautiful reverie, as he gives suck to the newborn infant inside him. He is engaged in blissful ruminations, in which he does not have to use his imagination at all, merely partaking of the most delirious maternal joy.

By contrast, the Conjugal Room is lawless, scatological, and filled with sexual extravaganza: "When he is sick, every man wants his mother; if she is not around, other mothers must do. Zuckerman was making do with four other women." They constitute the weepers, the love terrorists, the fault-finders, the avengers, and the hotsie-totsies. They are all fluent and fiery. This room is both cradle and battle-field. They represent ecstasy and nemesis. There is Faunia in *The Human Stain*, alas a loser; the rapacious Monkey in *Portnoy's Complaint*, to whom the protagonist, Portnoy, recites Yeats's "Leda and the Swan" at a torrid sexual junc-ture; and the majestically unhinged Maureen in *My Life as a Man*, for whom Roth seems to have a remaindered sneaking fondness.

"Whew. Have I got grievances," Portnoy says to his psy-chiatrist, in his raging, incessant spiel. Of the 430,000 citi-zens who bought the hardback, there were also a great tally of grievances. It was a repellent book, a burst of rage and romp, filled with fetid indiscretions and blasphemies, but most heinous of all was his vile depiction of women, both Jew and gentile. The author protested. He was not a screw-ball in search of catharsis, he was not a hating or avenging son, and his only crime was to have observed the human granules all around him and hone it into fiction. The impe-tus for the book came to him when he realized that Port-noy's guilt was a source of rich comedy. Moreover, he said to those disbelieving philistines, poor Alexander Portnoy was merely crying out for redemption.

Roth became famous overnight, accruing all the trap-pings and gossip and misconception that fame brings. He left New York and went to the Yaddo retreat for several months. From time to time he would send salvos back. It was not his intention to slither out of the slime, but rather to slide back into it. He was not interested in American pieties, propaganda, moral allegory, appeasement, or the conceits of the avant-garde about style, structure, symbolism, and so on.

He had said he was influenced by the mood of the sixties; the sexual liberation and pervasive theatricality emboldened him to write as he did, while at the same time, privately, he was expanding his concerns and his themes. He became more politicized, railed against Nixon's malevolent administration and, as he saw it, a president on the verge of mental disorder. As a citizen of America, the Vietnam War both appalled and mortified him. He went into seclusion and employed himself for many years, up in Connecticut, turning the sentences around and around, day by day, allowing himself a newspaper on Sundays, but with one proviso, that the Arts page be removed before the paper was delivered. He had cut himself off.

It is a moral and intellectual leap from *Portnoy's Complaint* to *American Pastoral*, and a more astonishing one to *Sabbath's Theater*. Naturally, there is the same merrymaking music of the transgressors, and Mickey Sabbath, the pagan puppeteer, does indeed dabble in the brackish waters of licentiousness, but he is also death-haunted, marked by the tragedies that occur both in war and peace, and ultimately wounded by great love and real loss.

Flaubert spoke of his Royal Room, where very few were admitted. For every writer, there is a writer who has gone before, who is both colossus and shadow. For Philip, that person—and therefore that guest—would be Kafka. He admired the great punitive fictions of *The Trial* and *The Metamorphosis*, but his favorite story is "The Burrow." A creature is building a vaulted chamber, a safe hole to hide in. His one tool is his forehead, just as a writer's one tool is the mind. The creature is joyous when blood flows. It means he has worked unrelentingly, and the walls are beginning to harden. Philip chose the story as a testament of how art is made. He depicts a portrait of the artist in all his ingenuity, anxiety, isolation, dissatisfaction, restlessness, secretiveness, self-addiction, and yet, the magical matter of a great story arising from all that human mess.

I visited Philip in many rooms over a period of thirty-six years. London, Connecticut, Essex House, where he and Claire lived for some time, and last of all, 79th Street. It was earlier this year. The change in him was almost imperceptible. The room had the same monastic neatness, books stacked everywhere, a larger pile on the table, close to where he sat, no flowers, no ornamentation, none of the empty liquor bottles such as John Berryman left in a hotel in Dublin, to where he had fled in an attempt to write. Propped on the hatch between the sitting room and the kitchen was a letter in a child's hand. It said: "Dear Mr. Roth, I would like to write a book with you."

Philip was as curious and as mischievous as ever. We laughed. To my chagrin, he told me how wealthy he was and how soundly he slept—"Like an angel." Yet the fire was dwindling. I do not say this in retrospect, but I did feel the relevance of Prospero's great line, which Philip had used as an epigram for *Sabbath's Theater*: "Every third thought shall be my grave."

It was raining and I could not stay long. Nor would he have wanted it. Time for his nap. He got out of his slippers and into his shoes.

"Don't come down with me . . . it's raining," I said.

"I'm coming down with you."

We stood on the step in the porch, while the doorman braved the taxi-mad supplicants. He looked up and down the street and said, almost boyishly, "I take a walk every day, try to be friendly, hi Joe, hi Phil, hi Nathan," and then more urgently he gripped my arm and said, "You're valiant, kid." It was not said in flattery, but rather as an incentive to keep going, to harden the walls of the burrow.

A taxi materialized, just in the nick of time. No more sentiment, no more laughs, no more anything.

Dear Mr. Roth, I would like to write a book with you.

Andrew Wylie

What Was Philip Really Like?

I N 1997, the year in which *American Pastoral* was published, my daughter, age twelve, wrote the following school essay.

A PHONE CALL FROM PHILIP ROTH

Ring ring ring ring
Ring ring ring ring
Ring ring ring ring . . .

I was watching television.
Hello?
Hello, Erica? It's Philip Roth. Is your Dad there?
No.
Can you take a message for me?
Yes.
Do you have a piece of paper?
Yes.
Do you have a pencil?
Yes.
OK, here's the message: It's Phiiiillliiip Roooooth. Do you have that? P-h-i-l-i-p – R-o-t-h.
Yes.
Philip Roth.

Yes.

OK, here's the message: Don't call back, I'm going to bed.

This was pure Philip. He was very careful, and never entirely confident that others would be as careful as he.

And why should he think they would be? It was unlikely. Things had to be *just right*. I paid very close attention to his instructions.

When I first began to work for Philip, he explained that there were few things he thoroughly understood, but he did know "how to publish Philip Roth. I have 20,000 readers. It doesn't matter what the book is, it will sell 20,000 copies. If I promote it, 20,000 copies. If I don't promote it, 20,000 copies. Between books, some of my readers die, and they're replaced by others, younger; but the number is always the same—20,000."

I told him that I thought perhaps we could increase that number. He was deeply skeptical. This was before *Sabbath's Theater, American Pastoral, I Married a Communist, The Human Stain*, and *The Plot Against America*.

He had been living for some time with Claire Bloom, and she was interested in marriage. Philip was not. He said, "I'll marry you when Nelson Mandela walks out of prison." Some time later, I was at home, watching Mandela's release. The phone rang.

It was Philip. "Are you watching this?"

"Yes."

"I'm fucked! I'm fucked! Get back in there, Mandela!"

Shortly afterwards, Philip and Claire were married. The marriage didn't last. He had these large books in mind—

the decades of American life. To write those great late books, he understood what was needed: isolation, concentration, hard work, and care. He would have to live alone. The work would have to be everything for him.

This kind of care was visible in his handwriting: the pen was at war with the paper, left hand curled around, pen pushed, shoved, forming jagged words.

And the care was also visible in his work. As he wrote, he would occasionally call to complain about how bad his work was, how difficult it was to get it right. "I'm no good at this, Andrew. It's killing me." Then he would revise . . . and revise . . . and revise . . . and revise . . . and revise.

It did not come easily. It took tremendous effort. He wrote standing up, on two upright desks at opposite sides of the writing room in Connecticut, separate from the house. He wore a path between those desks. In silence.

He was alone.

There was a telephone in that room. And I had the number. But it was for emergencies only, and I only used it once. If I wanted to speak to Philip routinely, I would send him a fax saying, "Please call Andrew." Sometimes the call came quickly, sometimes there was a delay.

The concentration was not to be broken. The focus was intense. He had the book mapped out in his mind. Later, he would get angry with Saul Bellow, when Saul could no longer hold a big book in his head.

And then, after the major novels were finished, something similar happened to Philip, and the last books were shorter, but equally concise. And then he stopped. It was about lacking strength, the physical power to continue writing.

He would quote Joe Louis: "I done the best I could with what I had." He claimed to be very happy not writing, and I believed him. He seemed content, right up to the end. He swam nearly every day.

Then on the day he died, he looked over at me and said, "Let me go. Let me go." It was the hardest instruction to follow.

Benjamin Taylor

I N *The Ghost Writer* Nathan Zuckerman says of Felix
Abravanel that the master's charm was "a moat so
oceanic that you could not even see the great turreted and
buttressed thing it had been dug to protect." Philip too
could seem a beguiling but remote citadel: august, many-
towered, lavishly defended. Those who reached the inner
keep met there someone quite different from the persona
devised for public purposes. Still vitally present at home
was the young man he'd remained all along, full of satirical
hijinks and gleeful ventriloquisms and antic fun building to
crescendos. Imaginary cousins were a specialty. I recall for
example Paprika Roth, a retired stripper living in the
Florida panhandle. A glint in the eye told you hilarity was
in the offing. "Ben, do you remember when Mrs. Fischbein
was on *The $64,000 Question*?"

"A little before my time, Philip."

"Well, Mrs. Fischbein had walloped the competition.
She'd advanced to the $64,000 question itself. Came the
drum roll and the announcer said, 'For $64,000, Mrs.
Fischbein, who was—the first man?' 'I wouldn't tell you for
a million dollars!' said Mrs. Fischbein."

The place of origin, Newark's Weequahic Section, much
spoken of here today, was his Great Code and Rosetta
Stone—I mean Weequahic as endlessly rediscovered through

alchemical imagination, that flame turned up under experience for the smelting of novels. "Ours was not a neighborhood steeped in darkness," says Zuckerman in *American Pastoral*.

> The place was bright with industriousness. There was a big belief in life and we were steered relentlessly in the direction of success; a better existence was going to be ours . . . Am I wrong to think we delighted in living there? No delusions are more familiar than those inspired in the elderly by nostalgia, but am I completely mistaken to think that living as well-born children in Renaissance Florence could not have held a candle to growing up within aromatic range of Tabachnik's pickle barrels? Am I mistaken to think that even back then, in the vivid present, the fullness of life stirred our emotions to an extraordinary extent? Has anywhere since so engrossed you in its ocean of details? The *detail*, the immensity of the detail, the force of the detail, the weight of the detail—the rich endlessness of detail surrounding you in your young life like the six feet of dirt that'll be packed on your grave when you're dead.

He spent his final three weeks in the cardiac intensive-care unit at New York–Presbyterian Hospital. Twelve days in, the attending came out of Philip's room and said to me: "He is philosopher, no?"

"Yes," I said. And so it really was. Amid the general weeping he was Socratic, as if instructing us, his loved ones, in how to die. He even remembered, like Socrates, a small debt owed—to Mrs. Salano, his housekeeper.

Near the end he asked for a moment alone with me and

said something I wrote down as soon as I decently could: "I have been to see the great enemy," he said, "and walked around him, and talked to him, and he is not to be feared. I promise."

There had been earlier brushes with the great enemy, any one of which might have proved fatal. Memory takes me back to Labor Day 2010. *Nemesis* was scheduled to appear that October. Once seated in our usual booth at the West Street Grill in Litchfield, which the management seemed to keep clear for him, we ordered the special soup, a gazpacho, sweet and crunchy with the local beefsteaks and cucumbers. I had a baseball question on the tip of my tongue: What was the name of "the natural," the player shot by a lady stalker in a Chicago hotel room? He gave me an amused look that darkened into puzzlement, then fear.

Then he pitched forward into the soup, unconscious. Too astounded for anything but composure, I summoned the management. Medics appeared almost immediately. As if by further magic a stretcher sprang up from the floor to receive Philip, who though all but comatose was saying something. An attempt—entirely characteristic—at instructing the medics, it sounded like.

A moment later I was in the front seat of the ambulance beside the driver, with Philip and the two medics behind us. "Thready pulse," said one to the other. And then, to the driver, "Better turn on the siren." And I thought, here is how it ends, and considered whom I would contact first. Thomas Mann's Aschenbach and the last line of *Death in Venice* came to mind, proving literature matters even in an emergency: "Before nightfall," writes Mann, "a shocked and respectful world received the news of his demise."

Twenty minutes after our arrival at Charlotte Hungerford Hospital in Torrington, the ER physician explained that what he had suffered was an accumulated reaction to one of the drugs he'd been taking. When I entered the examining room Philip said, "No more books." At first I didn't know what he meant. What he meant, I shortly realized, was that *Nemesis*, the thirty-first, would be his last. Thus he announced his retirement.

"You look right good for back from the dead," I told him.

"Just so we're clear," he said, "I did die." He had the sweetest smile sometimes. Now he took up the story he hadn't got to at dinner: In the summer of 1949 Eddie Waitkus, lefty All-Star with the Orioles, the Phillies, the Cubs, and the Phillies again, was shot by a deranged admirer, Ruth Ann Steinhagen, in her room at the Edgewater Beach Hotel, to which she'd coaxed him with a letter: "Please come soon. I won't take much of your time. I promise."

Good as her word, she plugged him when he came through the door. Ruth Ann's plan had evidently been to shoot herself too in a Mayerling-style bloodbath, but she told the cops afterward that she couldn't find another bullet.

Eddie survived but never got his game back. Ruth Ann reported that after she shot him he'd said: "What'd you do that for, baby?" He spent the rest of his days wondering, and died at fifty-three of esophageal cancer. Ruth Ann served a year in the madhouse at Kankakee and, released to the care of family, lived uneventfully on Chicago's North Side, turning away all queries till her death in 2012.

What proved evergreen was "What'd you do that for, baby?"—endlessly applicable and between Philip and me a fresh source of laughter each time one of us said it. Is the quick of friendship here, in finding the same things lastingly funny? Because it was he, because it was I? "Such a friendship has no model but itself," says Montaigne, "and can only be compared to itself . . . And is some mysterious quintessence . . ." Because it was he. Because it was I.

One of the many authors Philip read in those eight exuberant years of retirement was himself—everything from Brenda Patimkin asking Neil Klugman to hold her glasses through to Mr. Bucky Cantor instructing his playground charges, thirty books later, in how to throw the javelin. I believe he took a death-defying satisfaction in the vastness of what he'd wrought—a shelf of work augmenting the soul of the nation and built to outlast whatever unforeseeable chances and changes await us and our descendants. "And then he hurled the javelin," Philip wrote at journey's end.

> You could see each of his muscles bulging when he released it into the air. He let out a strangulated yowl of effort . . . a noise expressing the essence of him—the naked battle cry of striving excellence . . .
>
> We sent up a loud cheer and began leaping about. All of the javelin's trajectory had originated in Mr. Cantor's supple muscles. His was the body—the feet, the legs, the buttocks, the trunk, the arms, the shoulders, even the thick stump of the bull neck—that acting in unison had powered the throw. It was as though our playground director had turned into a primordial man,

hunting for food on the plains where he foraged, taming the wilds by the might of his hand. Never were we more in awe of anyone. Through him, we boys had left the little story of the neighborhood and entered the historical saga of our ancient gender.

He threw the javelin repeatedly that afternoon, each throw smooth and powerful, each throw accompanied by that resounding mingling of a shout and a grunt, and each, to our delight, landing several yards farther down the field than the last. Running with the javelin aloft, stretching his throwing arm back behind his body, bringing the throwing arm through to release the javelin high over his shoulder—and releasing it then like an explosion—he seemed to us invincible.

Joel Conarroe

Excerpts from Roth's Letters

AND say his glory was he had such friends. I know I speak for all of us when I thank our nine speakers for their eloquence and wit, for their insights into Philip's luminous body of work, and for their evocative memories. Thank you one and all!

I will let Philip have the last word, first with excerpts from letters during a year I spent in his Connecticut home, on a Guggenheim Fellowship, while he was in London. It was a magical time in which I had the gift not only of the glorious seasonal cycle but of access to his magnificent collection of books and music.

*   *   *

3/19/78 Come visit. I am forty-five today and half my life is now over. It will happen to you too soon. Don't waste your youth. Yours, at the midpoint, P

5/18/78 What do you mean no leaves? Get the f****** leaves! Get Bob [his handyman] to hang them up on the trees even before he puts the screens up. That is a must. I knew you'd screw up, Conarroe. The leaves for the maple tree by the studio are in the barn, behind the woodpile, and the leaves for the hawthorns are in New York. You'll have to drive down and get them from Jack Miles. I hope to f*** he hasn't sent them out to be cleaned—they were to be LAUN-DERED only. But I can't trust that guy either. De both of ye have driven me nuts. Philip

2/5/79 [*Julius Goldstein, a painter, one of Philip's closest friends, was married to Joan Aiken, a children's book writer. Julius was a source of fun for all of us who knew him, a role he relished. His nickname, as Barbara Sproul reminded me, was Señor Negativo, because he was an inspired kvetch.*]

Dear Cousin Gloucester, Come on over and see us. Garbage strike, hospital strike, train strike, and rumored strike of power workers. British Leyland is folding because of their strike. And on top of all that Goldstein is here. This place is liable now to prompt a complaint from him. We'll see when he comes Wednesday for dinner with Joan. Unless Joan is on strike. Your fed-up Yank, with British ways, Uncle Phil

Two weeks later he wrote: Goldstein was here during all the strikes. He seemed to think there was something wrong with England. At least to me that seemed the drift of his remarks.

2/29/79 You ate the chicken and corn that were in the freezer????? Our chicken and corn????? That we were saving for chicken and corn day when we got back????? You'll pay through the nose for that, Conarroe.

12/20/86 *When we were both in the States.* [*For young readers, "the Gipper" refers to Ronald Reagan.*]

Dear Joel, Ollie North is a Communist agent. I'm convinced of it. Why else would he have the same last name as the first name of both North Vietnam AND North Korea. THAT IS A CODE. He is a Communist spy. This has all been a great strain on the Gipper's prostate. Now we're going to find Bush wearing a dress in the men's room at Union Station in Washington. Those Commie bastards will stop at nothing. Your old Yank, PR

And here is Philip in a different tonality. On July 7, 2013, I asked, via email, whether he had seen an essay in The New York Times *by Oliver Sacks that managed, I suggested, to put words around what has often been thought but rarely so cogently expressed. Here is his response, which I had read so often I was able to recite from memory.*

Dear Joel, Thanks for putting me on to Sacks. Yes, he nails it. It's the damned poignancy of everything that rocks me a little. I see something beautiful or just altogether ordinary and I say to myself, "Take a good long look. Look at it as if you're never going to see it again because maybe you won't." It makes even one's familiar surroundings breathtaking, doesn't it? "Here I am," think I, "ambling happily into oblivion." The strategy I've been using on myself for decades now is that whenever death comes to mind in its most distressing form, I tell myself, quite simply, "I'm here and it's now," and those five little words do the trick. I'm here and it's now. So long as I'm alive I'm immortal, am I not? Now that writing's been over for close to four years, virtually every night I go to sleep with a goofy smile on my face and in the dark am made positively gleeful by softly uttering aloud, "I have recovered my life before I was embattled. The battles are over. I've come home. And I won." At twenty-three, I was discharged from the army badly compromised by the back injury I incurred there that was never to be through with me. At the University of Chicago, where I went to teach freshman composition, I almost immediately met Maggie, and, smart and self-possessed as I thought I was, stepped stupidly into the vortex of her scheming madness, and, what's more, I began publishing short stories that had the Jewish establishment howling at the top of its voice, to my family, my friends, and my fellow Jews that I was an anti-Semite and a self-hating Jew. Suddenly I was in a battle on three fronts. There were times in the years after when, despite the rewards of my career, which were close to instantaneous, I never thought I'd make it through the page I was writing, let alone come out the other end victorious. But I did. I won. "Look," Lawrence wrote, "we've come through." Isn't that what "awesome" used to mean? We came through. We came through.

At the conclusion of this letter we heard a recording of Gabriel Fauré's haunting Elegy in C Minor, which brought the memorial service to a close. We then gathered for a reception and a chance to share, amidst laughter and tears, memories of our beloved friend.—JC

Notes on the Contributors

Joel Conarroe, the author of books about American poets, is President Emeritus of the John Simon Guggenheim Memorial Foundation. He has served as Dean of Arts and Sciences at the University of Pennsylvania, as Executive Director of the Modern Language Association and editor of *PMLA*, as Chairman of the National Book Foundation, and as President of PEN.

Claudia Roth Pierpont is a staff writer for *The New Yorker* and the author of *Roth Unbound: A Writer and His Books*.

Norman Manea is a writer and Professor Emeritus and Distinguished Writer in Residence at Bard College.

Bernard Avishai is a Professor of Political Economy at Dartmouth College, the author of *Promiscuous: Portnoy's Complaint and Our Doomed Pursuit of Happiness*, and a regular contributor to *The New Yorker* online.

Nicole Kraus is a novelist and the author of *Man Walks into a Room*, *The History of Love*, *Great House*, and *Forest Dark*.

Janis Freedman Bellow teaches literature at Tufts University.

Judith Thurman won the National Book Award for her biography of Isak Dinesen, and the Los Angeles Times and Salon Book Awards for her biography of Colette. She is a longtime staff writer at *The New Yorker*.

Julia Golier is an Associate Professor of Psychiatry at the Mount Sinai School of Medicine and the Co-Literary Executor of the Estate of Philip Roth.

Edna O'Brien is a novelist, short story writer, and dramatist. She is an Honorary Member of the American Academy of Arts and Letters.

Andrew Wylie is a literary agent and the Co-Literary Executor of the Estate of Philip Roth.

Ben Taylor is a writer and a Trustee of the John Simon Guggenheim Memorial Foundation.

The Library of America Philip Roth Edition

Novels & Stories 1959–1962
Goodbye, Columbus and Five Short Stories • *Letting Go*

Novels 1967–1972
When She Was Good • *Portnoy's Complaint* • *Our Gang* •
The Breast

Novels 1973–1977
The Great American Novel • *My Life as a Man* •
The Professor of Desire

Zuckerman Bound: A Trilogy & Epilogue 1979–1985
The Ghost Writer • *Zuckerman Unbound* • *The Anatomy Lesson* •
The Prague Orgy • Previously unpublished television screenplay
for *The Prague Orgy*

Novels & Other Narratives 1986–1991
The Counterlife • *The Facts* • *Deception* • *Patrimony*

Novels 1993–1995
Operation Shylock • *Sabbath's Theater*

The American Trilogy 1997–2000
American Pastoral • *I Married a Communist* • *The Human Stain*

Novels 2001–2007
The Dying Animal • *The Plot Against America* • *Exit Ghost*

Nemeses
Everyman • *Indignation* • *The Humbling* • *Nemesis*

Why Write?
Collected Nonfiction 1960–2013

For more information, visit **www.loa.org/roth**.

This book is set in 11 point Minion Pro, a digital typeface
designed by Robert Slimbach in 1990 for Adobe Systems and
inspired by Renaissance-era fonts. The name comes from the
traditional nomenclature for type sizes, the smallest of which was
diamond, followed by pearl, agate, nonpareil, minion, brevier,
bourgeois, long primer, small pica, pica, etc.

The text paper is acid-free Glatfelter Offset; it exceeds the
requirements for permanence established by the American
National Standards Institute. The binding material is
Arrestox B-Cloth, a poly-cotton blend fabric with an
aqueous acrylic coating to resist stains and mildew.

Design and composition by
Library of America, New York, New York.

Printing and binding by
Thomson-Shore, Inc. Dexter, Michigan.